Artificial Intelligence

(A.I.) for Kids: The

Abiotic Brain

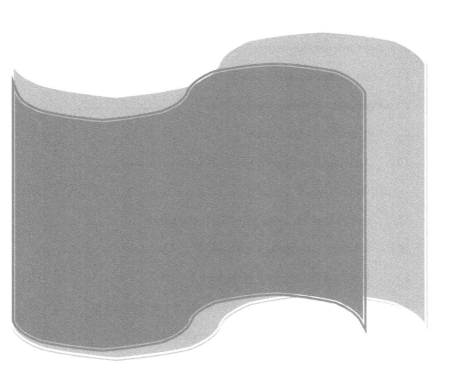

CONTENT

1. Global Recognition

https://favouriteblog.com/ai-kids-young-readers-tech/

https://www.parenting.com/shop/independently-published-artificial-intelligence-a-i-for-kids-the-abiotic-brain-pb9e16d5305d587b862bc5d2c72837b7d.html

https://www.quora.com/Is-there-any-good-Neural-network-or-AI-books-for-Kids-like-dummies-series-or-head-first-series-or-any-other-with-basic-coding-or-hardware-kits

https://kisslibrary.net/book/0DA4ECC833353FB168E5?utm_source=ps39&utm_medium=zimucogobody.tk&utm_campaign=fnom&x=7821013

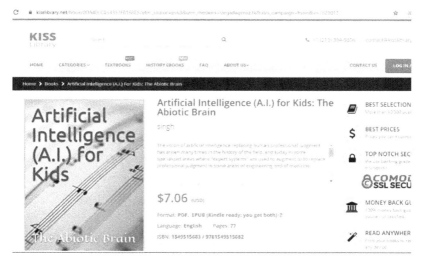

https://www.ebay.com/p/Artificial-Intelligence-A-I-for-Kids-The-Abiotic-Brain-by-singh-2017-Paperback/239584879

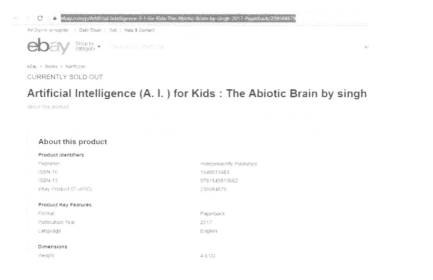

2. Introduction

Artificial Intelligence (also known simply as A.I.) is a 2001 American science fiction drama film directed by Steven Spielberg. Set in a futuristic post-climate change society, A.I. tells the story of David (Osment), a childlike android uniquely programmed with the ability to love.

Artificial Intelligence is something like "a machine replacing a man". The 21st century generation is now seeing a tremendous change in the environment. Right from an automated toothbrush detecting the germ presence to a machine that can detect a person's health needs and provide him timely advice as a part of diagnosis. In no time will we see that the robots will replace the man in every field.

Today, Schools are not preparing children to succeed in a world where intelligent robots have transformed the workforce.

Most of what people learn in school or in college will probably be irrelevant by the time they are 40 or 50. If they want to continue to have a job, and to understand the world, and be relevant to what is happening, people will have to reinvent themselves again and again, and faster and faster.

Once the mainstay of Sci-Fi films and novels, AI has crept into the technology sector and continues to expand in 2018. The field of AI was founded at a conference in 1956, however AI has become more widely known to the public audience during the past five to ten years.

Artificial Intelligence (AI) systems are transcending at an unprecedented rate. Digital marketing experts have predicted that in the next few years, fully automated AI systems will take over all the areas of marketing. The marketing strategies of many ecommerce businesses are going to be changed immensely by AI.

When machines actually will have ability like humans, most probably it will be based on the concept of programming like the human mind. They can think, make decisions, and have perceptions and beliefs. For instance the artificial intellectual supercomputer "WATSON" invented by IBM. Such AI does not currently exist however it is estimated by some experts that it may be developed by 2030 or 2045.

At present, machines behave like an intelligent human. Machines with such artificial intelligence have all abilities like thinking, moving, talking but are programmed to do so. In the chess game, the machine has the ability to play but it does not possess any thinking ability like humans. The machine is programmed to play chess and make smart moves to compete with other players

Responding to the economic effects of AI-driven automation will be a significant policy challenge for the next Administration and its successors. AI has already begun to transform the American workplace, changing the types of jobs available and the skills that workers need to thrive. All Americans should have the opportunity to participate in addressing these challenges, whether as students, workers, managers, or technical leaders, or simply as citizens with a voice in the policy debate.

More than two centuries ago, the Industrial Revolution was the most significant event in the human history since the domestication of animals and plants, leading to five decades of growth and development making the western world almost unrecognizable. Today the pace with which this disruptive technological revolution aided by AI is engulfing the humanity is not just swift, but almost exponential. In every decade and with much faster frequency in the days to come, we are wiping out our own inventions and innovations by terming them as obsolete.

AI raises many new policy questions, which should be continued topics for discussion and consideration by future Administrations, Congress, the private sector, and the public. Continued engagement among government, industry, technical and policy experts, and the public should play an important role in moving the Nation toward policies that create broadly shared prosperity, unlock the creative potential of American companies and workers, and ensure the Nation's continued leadership in the creation and use of AI.

If you're considering a voice-activated smart speaker for your office, the first question you may want to ask it is, "How secure are you?" Amazon, Google, Microsoft, and others offer an array of these smart speaker devices for use at home. These devices are activated by the user's voice and connect to the internet upon activation to play music, adjust the home's temperature, and answer questions, among other features. Companies are already advertising the benefits of these devices to businesses, where they could serve as a sort of virtual assistant. Amazon, for example, has launched Alexa for Business, suggesting the Alexa voice-activated devices can be used for everything from managing calendars to coordinating conference calls. However, the use of these devices in an office setting raises both privacy and security concerns.

Around the world, companies across industries are beginning to adopt the use of artificial intelligence (AI) and machine learning to massive advantage. Successful implementation of AI techniques holds the promise of revolutionary advances in how businesses operate—and of significant competitive advantages for early movers. But rates of AI adoption and success have not been equally distributed. One country, China, is currently well ahead of the rest of the industrialized world in AI implementation, with up to 85% of companies identifiable as "active players" in AI. Traditional powerhouses like Germany, while strong on AI research and infrastructure, are increasingly falling behind in actually leveraging the technology in practice.

The irony for many German companies is that they have worked hard for decades to establish a reputation for intelligently refining new innovations. The World Economic Forum's 2018 Global Competitiveness Report recently placed Germany at the top of the list in "innovation capability," ahead of the United States, China, and many others, based on its extensive academic research network and large volume of patents. Led in no small measure by tech-friendly sectors such as the automobile industry, German companies have historically learned to prosper by following a traditional approach to R&D—one that is deliberately incremental, thoroughly planned and research-driven, and frowns on trial and error. It is almost in these companies' DNA to take the long view and work diligently behind the scenes to perfect solutions to hard problems before launching them. But when it comes to technologies like AI, past innovation performance is no guarantee of future results. In fact, quite the opposite is true.

3. Evolution of Artificial Intelligence

The field of Artificial Intelligence (AI) was officially born and christened at a 1956 workshop organized by John McCarthy at the Dartmouth Summer Research Project on Artificial Intelligence. The goal was to investigate ways in which machines could be made to simulate aspects of intelligence—the essential idea that has continued to drive the field forward. McCarthy is credited with the first use of the term "artificial intelligence" in the proposal he co-authored for the workshop with Marvin Minsky, Nathaniel Rochester, and Claude Shannon. Many of the people who attended soon led significant projects under the banner of AI, including Arthur Samuel, Oliver Selfridge, Ray Solomonoff, Allen Newell, and Herbert Simon.

Although the Dartmouth workshop created a unified identity for the field and a dedicated research community, many of the technical ideas that have come to characterize AI existed much earlier. In the eighteenth century, Thomas Bayes provided a framework for reasoning about the probability of events. In the nineteenth century, George Boole showed that logical reasoning—dating back to

Aristotle—could be performed systematically in the same manner as solving a system of equations. By the turn of the twentieth century, progress in the experimental sciences had led to the emergence of the field of statistics, which enables inferences to be drawn rigorously from data. The idea of physically engineering a machine to execute sequences of instructions, which had captured the imagination of pioneers such as Charles Babbage, had matured by the 1950s, and resulted in the construction of the first electronic computers.

Primitive robots, which could sense and act autonomously, had also been built by that time.

The most influential ideas underpinning computer science came from Alan Turing, who proposed a formal model of computing. Turing's classic essay, Computing Machinery and Intelligence, imagines the possibility of computers created for simulating intelligence and explores many of the ingredients now associated with AI, including how intelligence might be tested, and how machines might automatically learn. Though these ideas inspired AI, Turing did not have access to the computing resources needed to translate his ideas into action.

Newell and Simon pioneered the foray into heuristic search, an efficient procedure for finding solutions in large, combinatorial spaces. In particular, they applied this idea to construct proofs of mathematical theorems, first through their Logic Theorist program, and then through the General Problem Solver. In the area of computer vision, early work in character recognition by Selfridge and colleagues laid the basis for more complex applications such as face recognition. By the late sixties, work had also begun on natural language processing. "Shakey", a wheeled robot built at SRI International, launched the field of mobile robotics. Samuel's Checkers-playing program, which improved itself through self-play, was one of the first working instances of a machine learning system. Rosenblatt's Perceptron, a computational model based on biological neurons, became the basis for the field of artificial neural networks. Feigenbaum and others advocated the case for building expert systems—knowledge repositories tailored for specialized domains such as chemistry and medical diagnosis.

Early conceptual progress assumed the existence of a symbolic system that could be reasoned about and built upon. But by the 1980s, despite this promising headway made into different aspects of artificial intelligence, the field still could boast no significant practical successes. This gap between theory and practice arose in part from an insufficient emphasis within the AI community on grounding systems physically, with direct access to environmental signals and data. There was also an overemphasis on Boolean (True/False) logic, overlooking the need to quantify uncertainty. The field was forced to take cognizance of these shortcomings in the mid-1980s, since interest in AI began to drop, and funding dried up. Nilsson calls this period the "AI winter."

A much needed resurgence in the nineties built upon the idea that "Good Old Fashioned AI" was inadequate as an end-to-end approach to building intelligent systems. Rather, intelligent systems needed to be built from the ground up, at all times solving the task at hand, albeit with different degrees of proficiency. Technological progress had also made the task of building systems driven by real-world data more feasible. Cheaper and more reliable hardware for sensing and actuation made robots easier to build. Further, the Internet's capacity for gathering large amounts of data, and the availability of computing power and storage to process that data, enabled statistical techniques that, by design, derive solutions from data. These developments have allowed AI to emerge in the past two decades as a profound influence on our daily lives.

4. Defining AI

Artificial intelligence, commonly abbreviated as AI, also known as machine intelligence, may be defined as "making a machine behave in ways that would be called intelligent if a human were so behaving". (John McCarthy, Proposal for the Dartmouth Summer Research Project On Artificial Intelligence.)

The term artificial intelligence (AI) refers to a set of computer science techniques that enable systems to perform tasks normally requiring human intelligence, such as visual perception, speech recognition, decision-making and language translation. Machine learning and deep learning are branches of AI which, based on algorithms and powerful data analysis, enable computers to learn and adapt independently. For ease of reference we will use "artificial intelligence", or AI, throughout this report to refer to machine learning, deep learning and other related techniques and technologies.

Since that time several distinct types of artificial intelligence have been elucidated:

Strong artificial intelligence deals with the creation of some form of computer-based artificial intelligence that can truly reason and solve problems; a strong form of AI is said to be sentient, or self-aware. In theory, there are two types of strong AI:

Human-like AI, in which the computer program thinks and reasons much like a human mind.

Non-human-like AI, in which the computer program develops a totally non-human sentience, and a non-human way of thinking and reasoning.

Weak artificial intelligence deals with the creation of some form of computer-based artificial intelligence that cannot truly reason and solve problems; such a machine would, in some ways, act as if it were intelligent, but it would not possesses true intelligence or sentience.

To date, much of the work in this field has been done with computer simulations of intelligence based on predefined sets of rules. Very little progress has been made in strong AI. Depending on how one defines one's goals, a moderate amount of progress has been made in weak AI.

Examples

Some of the A I examples around us are :

- LEGO Sudoku Bot: Are computers or humans better at Sudoku?

- Pancake Bot: Are computers better at making pancakes?

- Robot Dog: Are computers better at moving about?

- Robot Arm: Better at catching a something?

- Google Self-Driving Cars: And what about driving? (Note: the idea of "self-driving" relies heavily on what the experience of driving is like, which is non-trivially different if you are teaching in India versus Peru.)

5. Development of AI theory

Much of the (original) focus of artificial intelligence research draws from an experimental approach to psychology, and emphasizes what may be called linguistic intelligence (best exemplified in the Turing test).

Approaches to artificial intelligence that do not focus on linguistic intelligence include robotics and collective intelligence approaches, which focus on active manipulation of an environment, or consensus decision making, and draw from biology and political science when seeking models of how "intelligent" behaviour is organized.

Artificial intelligence theory also draws from animal studies, in particular with insects, which are easier to emulate as robots (see artificial life), or with apes, who resemble humans in many ways but have less developed capacities for planning and cognition. AI researchers argue that animals which are simpler than humans ought to be considerably easier to mimic.

Seminal papers advancing the concept of machine intelligence include A Logical Calculus of the Ideas

Immanent in Nervous Activity (1943), by Warren McCulloch and Walter Pitts, and On Computing Machinery and Intelligence (1950), by Alan Turing, and Man-Computer Symbiosis by J.C.R. Licklider.

There were also early papers which denied the possibility of machine intelligence on logical or philosophical grounds such as Minds, Machines and Gödel (1961) by John Lucas.

With the development of practical techniques based on AI research, advocates of AI have argued that opponents of AI have repeatedly changed their position on tasks such as computer chess or speech recognition that were previously regarded as "intelligent" in order to deny the accomplishments of AI. They point out that this moving of the goalposts effectively defines "intelligence" as "whatever humans can do that machines cannot".

John von Neumann (quoted by E.T. Jaynes) anticipated this in 1948 by saying, in response to a comment at a lecture that it was impossible for a machine to think: "You insist that there is something a machine cannot do. If you will tell me precisely what it is that a machine cannot do, then I can always make a machine which will do just that!". Von Neumann was presumably alluding to the Church-Turing thesis which states that any effective procedure can be simulated by a (generalized) computer.

1969 McCarthy and Hayes started the discussion about the frame problem with their essay, "Some Philosophical Problems from the Standpoint of Artificial Intelligence".

6.   Experimental AI research

How can scientists & engineers teach a robot to think? Will machines ever be smarter than humans? With simple text, diagrams, comic strip stories and stunning photographs, how intelligent machines can explore space, play games, create works of art, help surgeons and the armed forces, and lots more.

Major experimental research revolves around:

- how intelligence can be defined

- whether machines can 'think'

- sensory input in machine systems

- the nature of consciousness

- the controversial culturing of human neurons.

Artificial intelligence began as an experimental field in the 1950s with such pioneers as Allen Newell and Herbert Simon, who founded the first artificial intelligence laboratory at Carnegie-Mellon University, and McCarthy and Minsky, who founded the MIT AI Lab in 1959. They all attended the aforementioned Dartmouth College summer AI conference in 1956, which was organized by McCarthy, Minsky, and Nathan Rochester of IBM.

Historically, there are two broad styles of AI research - the "neats" and "scruffies". "Neat", classical or symbolic AI research, in general, involves symbolic manipulation of abstract concepts, and is the methodology used in most expert systems. Parallel to this are the "scruffy", or "connectionist", approaches, of which neural networks are the best-known example, which try to "evolve" intelligence through building systems and then improving them through some automatic process rather than systematically designing something to complete the task. Both approaches appeared very early in AI history. Throughout the 1960s and 1970s scruffy approaches were pushed to the background, but interest was regained in the 1980s when the limitations of the "neat" approaches of the time became clearer. However, it has become clear that contemporary methods using both broad approaches have severe limitations.

7. Practical applications of AI techniques

Success in creating AI would be the biggest event in human history. Unfortunately, it might also be the last, unless we learn how to avoid the risks.

Stephen Hawking

Whilst progress towards the ultimate goal of human-like intelligence has been slow, many spinoffs have come in the process. Notable examples include the languages LISP and Prolog, which were invented for AI research but are now used for non-AI tasks. Hacker culture first sprang from AI laboratories, in particular the MIT AI Lab, home at various times to such luminaries as McCarthy, Minsky, Seymour Papert (who developed Logo there), Terry Winograd (who abandoned AI after developing SHRDLU).

- Many other useful systems have been built using technologies that at least once were active areas of AI research. Some examples include:

- Deep Blue, a chess-playing computer, beat Garry Kasparov in a famous match in 1997.

- Fuzzy logic, a technique for reasoning under uncertainty, has been widely used in industrial control systems.

- Expert systems are being used to some extent industrially.

- Machine translation systems such as SYSTRAN are widely used, although results are not yet comparable with human translators.

- Neural networks have been used for a wide variety of tasks, from intrusion detection systems to computer games.

- Optical character recognition systems can translate arbitrary typewritten European script into text.

- Handwriting recognition is used in millions of personal digital assistants.

- Speech recognition is commercially available and is widely deployed.

- Computer algebra systems, such as Mathematica and Macsyma[?], are commonplace.

- Machine vision systems are used in many industrial applications.

The vision of artificial intelligence replacing human professional judgment has arisen many times in the history of the field, and today in some specialized areas where "expert systems" are used to augment or to replace professional judgment in some areas of engineering and of medicine.

8. Hypothetical consequences of AI

"Everything we love about civilization is a product of intelligence, so amplifying our human intelligence with artificial intelligence has the potential of helping civilization flourish like never before – as long as we manage to keep the technology beneficial." - **Max Tegmark**

Some observers foresee the development of systems that are far more intelligent and complex than anything currently known. One name for these hypothetical systems is artilects.

With the introduction of artificially intelligent non-deterministic systems, many ethical issues will arise. Many of these issues have never been encountered by humanity.

Over time, debates have tended to focus less and less on "possibility" and more on "desirability", as emphasized in the "Cosmist" (versus "Terran") debates initiated by Hugo De Garis and Kevin Warwick. A Cosmist, according to de Garis, is actually seeking to build more intelligent successors to the human species. The emergence of this debate suggests that desirability questions may also have influenced some of the early thinkers "against".

Some issues that bring up interesting ethical questions are:

- Determining the sentience of a system we create.

- Turing test

- Cognition

Why do we have a need to categorize these systems at all Freedoms and rights for these systems. Designing systems that are far more impressive than any one human. Deciding how much safe-guards to design into these systems. Seeing how much learning capability a system needs to replicate human thought, or how well it could do tasks without it (e.g., expert system)

9. Sub-fields of AI research

I definitely fall into the camp of thinking of AI as augmenting human capability and capacity.

Satya Nadella

- Combinatorial search
- Computer vision
- Expert system
- Genetic programming
- Genetic algorithm
- Knowledge representation
- Machine learning
- Machine planning
- Neural network
- Natural language processing
- Robotics
- Artificial life
- Distributed Artificial Intelligence

Computer programs displaying some degree of "intelligence"

- ALICE

- ELIZA (demonstration of limits of AI)

- Hal

- Mind-1.1

Some of the milestones in the development of AI are:

A. Search and Planning deal with reasoning about goal-directed behavior. Search plays a key role, for example, in chess-playing programs such as Deep Blue, in deciding which move (behavior) will ultimately lead to a win (goal).

B. The area of Knowledge Representation and Reasoning involves processing information (typically when in large amounts) into a structured form that can be queried more reliably and efficiently. IBM's Watson program, which beat human contenders to win the Jeopardy challenge in 2011, was largely based on an efficient scheme for organizing, indexing, and retrieving large amounts of information gathered from various sources

C. Machine Learning is a paradigm that enables systems to automatically improve their performance at a task by observing relevant data. Indeed, machine learning has been the key contributor to the AI surge in the past few decades, ranging from search and product recommendation engines, to systems for speech recognition, fraud detection, image understanding, and countless other tasks that once relied on human skill and judgment. The automation of these tasks has enabled the scaling up of services such as e-commerce.

D. As more and more intelligent systems get built, a natural question to consider is how such systems will interact with each other. The field of Multi-Agent Systems considers this question, which is becoming increasingly important in on-line marketplaces and transportation systems.

E. From its early days, AI has taken up the design and construction of systems that are embodied in the real world. The area of Robotics investigates fundamental aspects of sensing and acting—and especially their integration—that enable a robot to behave effectively. Since robots and other computer systems share the living world with human beings, the specialized subject of Human Robot Interaction has also become prominent in recent decades.

F. Machine perception has always played a central role in AI, partly in developing robotics, but also as a completely independent area of study. The most commonly studied perception modalities are Computer Vision and Natural Language Processing, each of which is attended to by large and vibrant communities.

G. Several other focus areas within AI today are consequences of the growth of the Internet. Social Network Analysis investigates the effect of neighborhood relations in influencing the behavior of individuals and communities.

Crowdsourcing is yet another innovative problem-solving technique, which relies on harnessing human intelligence (typically from thousands of humans) to solve hard computational problems.

10. Artificial intelligence in literature and movies

Many smart people predict AI for the foreseeable future will play an assistive role for humans, which is how robots have been portrayed in popular literature and films for
decades, from Robby the Robot in the 1956 film Forbidden Planet to R2-D2 and C-3PO in the Star Wars movies.

- HAL 9000 in 2001 A Space Odyssey
- A.I.: Artificial Intelligence

Artificial intelligence -- mainly its philosophical implications and its impact on the humanities -- is a major theme in David Lodge's campus novel Thinks ... (2001).

- Mike in The Moon is a Harsh Mistress by Robert A. Heinlein
- Neuromancer
- Various novels by Isaac Asimov
- Ghost in the Shell
- The Matrix

- The Terminator series

Speculative non-fiction books about artificial intelligence

- The Age of Spiritual Machines

Learn More

- AI Depot (http://ai-depot.com/) -- community discussion, news, and articles

- Loebner Prize website (http://www.loebner.net/Prizef/loebner-prize)

- AIWiki (http://purl.net/net/AIWiki) - a wiki devoted entirely to Artificial Intelligence.

11. List of Movies using Artificial Intelligence

Period	Movie Title	AI References
1927	Metropolis	Maria's robot double
1934	Der Herr der Welt (i.e. Master of the World)	Überroboter / Kampfmaschine (i.e. fighting machine), working-robots
1951	The Day the Earth Stood Still	Gort
1957	The Invisible Boy	Robby the Robot
1965	Alphaville	Alpha 60
1968	2001: A Space Odyssey	HAL 9000
1970	Colossus: The Forbin Project	Colossus, Guardian
1973	Westworld	
1977	Demon Seed	Proteus IV
1977	Star Wars	R2-D2, C-3PO
1979	Star Trek: The Motion Picture	V'Ger
1979	Alien	
1982	Blade Runner	Replicants
1982	Airplane II	
1982	Tron	Master Control Program
1983	Superman III	Supercomputer
1983	WarGames	WOPR (War Operation Plan Response), Joshua
1984	Electric Dreams	Edgar
1984	Hide and Seek	P-1
1984	The Terminator	Skynet, the Terminator
1985	D.A.R.Y.L.	Daryl
1986	Short Circuit	Number 5, Johnny Five
1987	RoboCop	RoboCop, Murphy
1988	Short Circuit 2	Number 5, Johnny Five

1991	Terminator 2: Judgment Day	Skynet, the Terminator, T-1000, T-800
1994	Star Trek Generations	Data
1995	Ghost in the Shell	The Puppet Master
1995	Mighty Morphin Power Rangers: The Movie	Alpha 5, Zordon, Zords
1996	Star Trek First Contact	Data, The Borg
1997	Austin Powers: International Man of Mystery	
1997	Nirvana	Solo
1999	The Iron Giant	
1999	The Matrix	Agents, Sentinels
1999	Bicentennial Man	Andrew Martin
1999	Star Wars: Episode I - The Phantom Menace	battle droids, C-3PO and R2-D2
2001	A.I. Artificial Intelligence	David, Gigolo Joe, Teddy
2002	Star Wars: Episode II - Attack of the Clones	battle droids, C-3PO and R2-D2
2002	Resident Evil	Red Queen
2002	S1M0NE	Simone
2003	The Matrix Reloaded	Agents, Sentinels
2003	Terminator 3: Rise of the Machines	Skynet, the Terminator, T-X
2003	The Matrix Revolutions	Agents, Sentinels
2004	I, Robot	VIKI (Virtual Interactive Kinetic Intelligence), Sonny
2005	The Hitchhiker's Guide to the Galaxy	Marvin the Paraonid Android, Deep Thought, Eddie the Computer
2005	Star Wars: Episode III - Revenge of the Sith	battle droids, C-3PO and R2-D2
2005	Stealth	EDI
2007	Resident Evil: Extinction	White Queen
2008	Eagle Eye	Autonomous Reconnaissance Intelligence Integration Analyst (ARIIA)
2008	Iron Man	JARVIS (Just A Rather Very Intelligent System)
2008	WALL-E	WALL-E
2008	The Day the Earth Stood Still (2008 film)	Gort

2009	Terminator Salvation	Skynet, the Terminator
2009	Moon	GERTY
2010	Tron: Legacy	
2010	Enthiran	Chitti the Robot
2011	Eva	Eva, Max, SI-9
2011	Real Steel	
2011	Ra.One	Ra.One,G.One
2012	Prometheus	David
2012	Resident Evil: Retribution	Red Queen
2012	Robot & Frank	Robot
2012	Total Recall	
2013	Her	Samantha
2013	Iron Man 3	JARVIS, Iron Legion
2013	The Machine	Machine
2013	Pacific Rim	A.I., Jaegers
2013	Elysium	Elysium robots
2014	Automata	
2014	Big Hero 6	Baymax
2014	Interstellar	TARS and CASE
2014	Robocop (2014 film)	RoboCop, Murphy
2014	Transcendence	Dr. Will Caster
2014	Transformers: Age of Extinction	Autobots, Decepticons, Dinobots
2014	X-Men: Days of Future Past	Sentinels
2015	Ex Machina	Ava
2015	Chappie	Chappie
2015	Tomorrowland	Athena and other robots
2015	Avengers: Age of Ultron	Iron Legion, Veronica, Hulkbuster, Ultron, JARVIS, Vision
2015	Terminator Genisys, aka Terminator 5	T-800, T-1000, T-3000, Skynet, Genisys
2015	Star Wars: The Force Awakens	BB-8, C-3PO and R2-D2
2015	Uncanny	
2015	Psycho-pass: The Movie	Sibyl System
2016	Max Steel	Steel
2016	Morgan	Morgan, Lee Weathers

2016	Resident Evil: The Final Chapter	Red Queen
2016	Rogue One: A Star Wars Story	K-2SO
2016	Infinity Chamber	Howard
2016	Passengers (2016 film)	Ship androids
2017	Power Rangers	Alpha 5, Zordon, Zords
2017	Spider-Man: Homecoming	Karen
2017	Ghost in the Shell (2017 film)	Motoko Kusanagi
2017	Transformers: The Last Knight	Autobots, Decepticons, Dinobots
2017	Alien: Covenant	David
2017	Blade Runner 2049	Replicants
2017	Star Wars: The Last Jedi	BB-8, C-3PO and R2-D2
2018	Upgrade	
2018	Zoe	Ash
2018	Tau	Tau
2018	Avengers: Infinity War	Vision
2018	2036 Origin Unknown	

Language is one of the most complex things for computers to understand. Guessing how to complete a sentence is pretty easy for people but much more difficult for machines. Historically, computers have been able to predict simple words like "on" or "at" and verbs like "run" or "eat", but they don't do as well at predicting nouns like "ball", "table" or people's names.

Artificial intelligence (AI) is either the greatest thing to ever happen to human work or the dread of our existence. Like most polarizing topics, the truth typically resides somewhere in the middle.

12. Artificial intelligence in Fashion

For a growing number of fashion companies, artificial Intelligence is already transforming the methods used to predict trends, create products and interact with suppliers and customers. Can there really be an algorithm for style? Surely not.

In 2003, Kate Moss found a lemon-yellow 50s chiffon dress in Lily et Cie, a vintage store in Beverly Hills, and wore it to a dinner at New York fashion week, where the entire room fell in love with it and a million copycat versions were born. The dress wasn't in keeping with that season's catwalk trends, or colours, but it was somehow absolutely right for that moment. It was like serendipity, like magic. How would an algorithm replace the je ne sais quoi of Kate Moss? Or Jane Birkin in the south of France with Serge, or Bianca Jagger at Studio 54?

In an era of "fast fashion" and online influencers, designers, suppliers and retailers are under constant pressure to predict what consumers want and make it available almost instantaneously. Trends change within weeks or even days, not just a few times a year. While companies have access to large volumes of data about both individual consumers and entire markets, from sales figures to social media feeds to customer product reviews, human beings can't process all this data quickly enough for it to be useful, and their conclusions are inevitably influenced by their own biases and preferences. In the 21st century, technology is defining our taste.

Ten years after its launch, Airbnb is not just a platform to rent somewhere to stay, but a silent tastemaker which has drawn a template for how a desirable home should look. White or bright accent walls, raw wood, Nespresso machines, Eames chairs, patterned rugs on bare floors, open shelving, Scandi-chic, the industrial look, and a minimal version of mid-century were characteristics that Kyle Chakya identified as the Airbnb "look" two years ago.

Standardisation evolved organically, as would-be hosts copied the look of the most popular spaces on the site. And then renters taken by the bare Edison lightbulbs and gallery walls of black and white photography in homes they stayed in while on holiday began to bring the look into their own homes. It is easy to imagine a similar process taking place in our wardrobes, once facsimile style advice is being beamed into each of our homes.

The robots are not necessarily the bad guys. Artificial intelligence could hold the key to making fashion more sustainable. "We are producing too much clothing and throwing away too much clothing," says Matthew Drinkwater, head of the Fashion Innovation Agency at the London College of Fashion.

Hilfiger also uses IBM's AI technology to analyze sales performance and customer reviews for each item in its collections and to predict future trends— and to aid in designing its collections. The available technology includes a color analysis tool, silhouette recognition tool and print tool, all of which allow human designers to access and combine vast numbers of images for inspiration. The software tools do the time-consuming work of analyzing trends and compiling data, allowing designers to focus on the creative process.

1. "The retail model needs to change. AI makes it possible to adjust manufacture in real time, responding to customer design as it happens, so that waste is minimised." The opportunities for personalisation – from monograms to

bespoke tailoring using 3D measurements taken online – hold the promise of clothes that we will value more, and wear for longer.

13. Artificial intelligence in Politics

AI innovation is moving at a rapid pace, and governments are currently scrambling to define strategies to ensure that their economies are not left behind. Many companies themselves are vocal in calling for national investments and for incentive schemes, in the expectation that this will "spark AI" in their businesses. Indeed, structural improvements at the national level do play an important role in laying the foundations for AI growth—investments in data infrastructure, in research hubs and networks, and in higher education for IT and data-related fields.

AI technologies are already being used by political actors in gerrymandering and targeted "robocalls" designed to suppress votes, and on social media platforms in the form of "bots." They can enable coordinated protest as well as the ability to predict protests, and promote greater transparency in politics by more accurately pinpointing who said what, when. Thus, administrative and regulatory laws regarding AI can be designed to promote greater democratic participation or, if ill-conceived, to reduce it. This list is not exhaustive and focuses largely on domestic policy in the United States, leaving out many areas of law that AI is likely to touch.

One lesson that might be drawn concerns the growing disconnect between the context-specific way in which AI is governed today and a wider consideration of themes shared by AI technologies across industries or sectors of society. It could be tempting to create new institutional configurations capable of amassing expertise and setting AI standards across multiple contexts.

2. Policymakers should recognize that to varying degrees and over time, various industries will need distinct, appropriate, regulations that touch on software built using AI or incorporating AI in some way. The government will need the expertise to scrutinize standards and technology developed by the private and public sector, and to craft regulations where necessary.

14. Can computers ever become as smart as humans?

"I believe there is no deep difference between what can be achieved by a biological brain and what can be achieved by a computer. It therefore follows that computers can, in theory, emulate human intelligence — and exceed it." - **Stephen Hawking**

Self-driving cars offer a good example of the amount of work that needs to go in before AI systems can reach human level intelligence. Because there are things that humans understand when approaching certain situations that would be difficult to teach to a machine. In a long blog post on autonomous cars, Rodney Brooks brings up a number of such situations, including how an autonomous car might approach a stop sign at a cross walk in a city neighborhood with an adult and child standing at the corner chatting. The algorithm would probably be tuned to wait for the pedestrians to cross, but what if they had no intention of crossing because they were waiting for a school bus? A human driver could signal to the pedestrians to go, and they in turn could wave the car on, but a driverless car could potentially be stuck there endlessly waiting for the pair to cross because they have no understanding of these uniquely human signals.

But one thing is certain. Given the recent developments in the field of AI, there will come a day when humans will not be the smartest entity on this planet. What happens then? Will computers annihilate humans or continue to serve them? And how can we put safeguards in place?

One option is to find market solutions, putting up money to fund research in ethical and safe AI, as Musk has done with OpenAI. The other is more dangerous. At a gathering of US governors earlier this month, Musk pressed them to "be proactive about regulation". What precisely does that entail? Pure research and their practical applications interact constantly to push the field of AI and robotics forward. Government control and red tape to stave off a vague, imprecise threat would be an innovation-killer.

"The rise of powerful AI will be either the best, or the worst thing, ever to happen to humanity. We do not yet know which." – **Stephen Hawking**

One of the most important technological advancements of the 21st century is the integration of computers into almost all aspects of our lives. Computer scientists develop powerful software and algorithms that have the incredible predictive power to match products to consumers, predict political elections, and even help people find lifelong romantic partners. They also create software that powers AI, which has led to extremely good facial and voice recognition and even self-driving vehicles. As our ability to collect and process ever larger amounts of data grows, so will the importance of computer scientists.

15. AI for Cyber Defence and Fraud Detection

Currently, designing and operating secure systems requires a large investment of time and attention from experts. Automating this expert work, partially or entirely, may enable strong security across a much broader range of systems and applications at dramatically lower cost, and may increase the agility of cyber defenses. Using AI may help maintain the rapid response required to detect and react to the landscape of ever evolving cyber threats. There are many opportunities for AI and specifically machine-learning systems to help cope with the sheer complexity of cyberspace and support effective human decision making in response to cyberattacks.

Future AI systems could perform predictive analytics to anticipate cyberattacks by generating dynamic threat models from available data sources that are voluminous, ever-changing, and often incomplete. These data include the topology and state of network nodes, links, equipment, architecture, protocols, and networks.

AI may be the most effective approach to interpreting these data, proactively identifying vulnerabilities, and taking action to prevent or mitigate future attacks. Results to-date in DARPA's Cyber Grand Challenge competition demonstrate the potential of this approach. The Cyber Grand Challenge was designed to accelerate the development of advanced, autonomous systems that can detect, evaluate, and patch software vulnerabilities before adversaries have a chance to exploit them. The Cyber Grand Challenge Final Event was held on August 4, 2016. To fuel follow-on research and parallel competition, all of the code produced by the automated systems during the Cyber Grand Challenge Final Event has been released as open source to allow others to reverse engineer it and learn from it.

AI also has important applications in detecting fraudulent transactions and messages. AI is widely used in the industry to detect fraudulent financial transactions and unauthorized attempts to log in to systems by impersonating a user. AI is used to filter email messages to flag spam, attempted cyberattacks, or otherwise unwanted messages. Search engines have worked for years to maintain the quality of search results by finding relevant features of documents and actions, and developing advanced algorithms to detect and demote content that appears to be unwanted or dangerous. In all of these areas, companies regularly update their methods to counter new tactics used by attackers and coordination among attackers.

Companies could develop AI-based methods to detect fraudulent transactions and messages in other settings, enabling their users to experience a higher-quality information environment.

Further research is needed to understand the most effective means of doing this.

16. Biotic

Scientists call living things in an ecosystem biotic elements. Nonliving things in ecosystems are abiotic elements such as rocks, soil, and water. Biotic elements have five basic needs for survival. Most biotic elements — polar bears, mosquitoes, dandelions, maple trees, and you — need these same five basic things: 1. oxygen 2. water 3. food 4. energy 5. suitable habitat (place to live)

- The inflammatory response to mosquito bites on a moose.

- A monkey's blood clotting mechanism during the initiation of an open wound.

- The zero volume increase of bird lungs during their breaths.

- The super high muscle twitch rate of an ordinary house fly's wings.

- The incredible liquid force (pressure) coming out of the blue whale's heart during atrial compression.

- The ossification of the shoulder bone on a lemur monkey.

- The growth process of the human brain during week 25 of pregnancy.

- The movement of an amoeba through pond water by changing the shape of their body, forming pseudopods.

- The reproduction rate of Clostridium perfringens, one of the fastest-growing bacteria, having a re-generation time of about 10 minutes.

- Number 10 of biotic example is below. The incredible rotating beauty of the ATP synthase molecule in all living things. Seriously, see the video, below. It is amazing.

17. *Abiotic*

- Water melting from a cool looking ice sculpture into a puddle below.

- Milk going sour after the expiration date.

- The formation of the Grand Canyon.

- The almost uncountable number of moons encircling Jupiter.

- The vast size of the Milky Way galaxy.

- A Van Gogh painting's changing color ever so slowly over time as the yellow paint he used decays.

- The time between the pitch drop in the drip experiment.

- The coloring of the Iron (Fe) molecule to red when it is attached to an Oxygen molecule.

- The coloring of concrete over time.

- The growth of zinc whiskers in outer space on human satellites.

18. When Abiotic meets Biotic

Elon Musk is worried about AI apocalypse, but I am worried about people losing their jobs. The society will have to adapt to a situation where people learn throughout their lives depending on the skills needed in the marketplace.

Andrew Ng

Plants use sunlight, soil, and water to grow. Animals use leaves, branches, trees, or soil for shelter and other living things for food. These are examples of interactions of biotic and abiotic elements in ecosystems. In a pond, the plants, soil, and water create suitable habitat for many different birds, insects, and fish. Some animals, such as deer, eat plants. Other animals, such as bears, eat fish and berries. Feeding interactions give living things the nutrients they need to survive.

One common interaction between biotic and abiotic components of an ecosystem is photosynthesis. Sunlight is abiotic (solely energy), and it fuels the synthesis of sugars and proteins inside plant cells once it is taken up by plant leaves.

In general, biotic factors are the living components of an ecosystem and are sorted into three groups: producers or autotrophs, consumers or heterotrophs, and decomposers or detritivores. Examples of biotic factors include: Grass as producers (autotrophs).

Abiotic factors are all of the non-living things in an ecosystem. Abiotic factors come in all shapes and sizes. They can be as small as a rock or as large as the sun.

19. Scope of AI

Building advanced AI is like launching a rocket. The first challenge is to maximize acceleration, but once it starts picking up speed, you also need to focus on steering.

Jaan Tallinn

Bill Gates believes there's reason to be cautious, but that the good can outweigh the bad if managed properly. Since recent developments have made super-intelligent machines possible much sooner than initially thought, the time is now to determine what dangers artificial intelligence poses. Artificial intelligence is the engineering and science of making intelligent machines and intelligent computer programs. Artificial intelligence is different from psychology because it emphasis on computation and is different from computer science because of its emphasis on perception, reasoning and action.

Artificial Intelligence is to develop intelligence in the machines or software and provide them the ability to think as humans. John McCarthy is known as the father of Artificial Intelligence. Artificial intelligence is based on various disciplines of a science and technology such as Biology Computer

Science, Psychology, Linguistics, Mathematics, and Engineering.

Companies can utilize the AI machines algorithms to identify patterns and insights in the huge amount of data.AI can help them take decision faster and improve their position in the competitive business world. Gartner stated that more than 85% of customer interactions will be managed without a human by 2020.

Robots

Robots embedded with sensors such as sound, bump, pressure, heat, light and temperature can detect the physical data and perform the instructions by a human. They have efficient processors and huge memory to make smart decisions and exhibit intelligence. Intelligent Robots are also capable to learn from mistakes.

Software

The handwriting recognition software acquires the data through the text written on paper or on screen. This software then recognizes the pattern in handwriting like shapes of letters and the text is then converted to editable text

Entertainment

AI based apps like Spotify, Pandora, and Netflix recommend music and movies based on the interests of users and their past choices. This data collected is then fed into AI learning algorithm to suggest recommendations.

Medicine

AI application in healthcare lies in Diabetic Retinopathy Treatment, Medical Diagnosis, Risk Prediction and Automating Drug Discovery. For example, In Skin Cancer Treatment Sebastian Thrun''s lab at Stanford released an AI algorithm which detects Skin Cancer with very high accuracy.

Games

Machines can now compete with humans in games with artificial intelligence.AI implementation can be seen in many strategic games such as poker, chess, tic-tac-toe, etc. Machines are empowered with ability to think of many positions based on heuristic knowledge. Deep Blue was the first a chess-playing computer developed by IBM. Other example is of Google"s AlphaGo.AI Go player has defeated Ke Jie, Go world champion.

Mobility

3. Autonomous transportation will soon be commonplace and, as most people's first experience with physically embodied AI systems, will strongly influence the public's perception of AI. As cars become better drivers than people, city-dwellers will own fewer cars, live further from work, and spend time differently, leading to an entirely new urban organization. In the typical North American city in 2030, physically embodied AI applications will not be limited to cars, but are likely to include trucks, flying vehicles, and personal robots. Improvements in safe and reliable hardware will spur innovation over the next fifteen years, as they will with Home/Service Robots, which have already entered people's houses, primarily in the form of vacuum cleaners. Better chips, low-cost 3D sensors, cloud-based machine learning, and advances in speech understanding will enhance future robots' services and their interactions with people. Special purpose robots will deliver packages, clean offices,

and enhance security. But technical constraints and the high costs of reliable mechanical devices will continue to limit commercial opportunities to narrowly defined applications for the foreseeable future.

20. Future of Artificial Intelligence

Legendary physicist Stephen Hawking, Tesla and SpaceX leader and innovator Elon Musk suggest that Artificial Intelligence could potentially be very dangerous. US government said in Dec 2016 in one of the official report , "Advances in Artificial Intelligence (AI) technology and related fields have opened up new markets and new opportunities for progress in critical areas such as health, education, energy, economic inclusion, social welfare, and the environment. In recent years, machines have surpassed humans in the performance of certain tasks related to intelligence, such as aspects of image recognition. Experts forecast that rapid progress in the field of specialized artificial intelligence will continue. Although it is unlikely that machines will exhibit broadly-applicable intelligence comparable to or exceeding that of humans in the next 20 years, it is to be expected that machines will continue to reach and exceed human performance on more and more tasks."

Accelerating artificial intelligence (AI) capabilities will enable automation of some tasks that have long required human labor.1 These transformations will open up new opportunities for individuals, the economy, and society, but they have the potential to disrupt the current livelihoods of millions of Americans. Whether AI leads to unemployment and increases in inequality over the long-run depends not only on the technology itself but also on the institutions and policies that are in place.

Recent progress in Artificial Intelligence (AI) has brought renewed attention to questions about automation driven by these advances and their impact on the economy. The current wave of progress and enthusiasm for AI began around 2010, driven by three mutually reinforcing factors: the availability of big data from sources including e-commerce, businesses, social media, science, and government; which provided raw material for dramatically improved machine learning approaches and algorithms; which in turn relied on the capabilities of more powerful computers. During this period, the pace of improvement surprised AI experts. For example, on a popular image recognition challenge that has a 5 percent human error rate according to one error measure, the best AI result improved from a 26 percent error rate in 2011 to 3.5 percent in 2015. This progress may enable a range of workplace tasks that require image understanding to be automated, and will also enable new types of work and jobs. Progress on other AI challenges will drive similar economic changes.

21. Way Forward

The goal of AI applications must be to create value for society. Strategies that enhance our ability to interpret AI systems and participate in their use may help build trust and prevent drastic failures. Care must be taken to augment and enhance human capabilities and interaction, and to avoid discrimination against segments of society.

Throughout history, humans have both shaped and adapted to new technologies. Scientists and academics sat up and took notice in 2016 when Alpha Go, Google DeepMind's AI-driven computer, won its five-match series against Lee Sedol, the reigning world champion in Go, the ancient Asian board game.

Business leaders should also have paid heed. Alpha Go's victory demonstrated in a very public way the learning capacity that AI-based technologies now possess. Humans didn't teach the computer—it taught itself how to master the game by playing it millions of times with another computer (through a set of techniques called "deep learning"), and independently responded to Mr Lee's moves.

Machine learning, a subcategory of AI techniques which automate the learning process through algorithms and the super-powered analysis of data, has been around since the 1950s. Business applications were trialled in the financial industry as early as the 1980s but did not go far. In recent years, advances in science combined with huge increases in (and declining prices of) computing power, swelling oceans of data and increasingly sophisticated analytics have for all practical purposes made machine learning and AI business-ready. It also helps that expertise in the field is now available to companies. "AI was very difficult to do for most companies until now partly because the number of experts in the field was extremely small," explains Yann LeCun, director of AI research at Facebook, a social media giant. "This shortage is easing, as even young graduates now have knowledge of AI techniques. There are also tools and platforms being built for people who are not yet experts to get started on developing AI applications."

If AI realises its business potential in the next 3-5 years, there is little question that it will lead to significant improvements in processes, as well as in the precision and reliability, and possibly the speed, of operational business decisions. AI is also more likely to enhance security and improve risk management than to weaken them, although some have concerns about AI's potential misuse.

The greatest risks that AI poses to companies probably lie less in its potential for disruption, and more in the unknowns surrounding it. After all, AI has only recently made it out of the laboratory, and business leaders are only now realising its commercial potential. Scientists believe there is a long way to go before they even scratch the surface of AI's capabilities. It cannot be discounted that AI will take businesses and industries in directions they do not want to go. But its future development is at least as likely to uncover new and exciting applications that will benefit companies and consumers alike.

Face recognition, self-driving cars, industrial robots, tumor detection and automated sport journalism are all real-world enigmas being solved with applications of intelligence (AI.) Today AI applications focus on very narrow tasks, but together these AI-driven tasks are reshaping businesses, industries and markets as the technology becomes more sophisticated, the use of AI will continue to grow quickly in the coming years.

AI is widely known in sports industry and is shaping the industry at a fast pace. AI is not only used to track player statistics but also by teams and organizations to enrich the fan experience.

Gartner predicts that 85% of interactions between customers and retailers will happen "without interacting with a human" by 2020. How can online retailers adapt to consumer-driven demand for more automation, and how will it be beneficial?

Saudi Arabia became the first country to grant citizenship to a being of Artificial Intelligence, and the robot, named Sophia, made headlines with her citizenship.

Google's facial tagging technology was logging black people as gorillas, and (debunked) rumours circulated that Facebook had pulled its chatbots, which had learnt to lie, because they had gotten too clever.

But AI's real successes have been fewer sensationalists in the public eye, and we're beginning to see how AI can be incorporated into e-commerce, both to enhance consumer experience and to attract users into accessing your platform, increasing conversion rates.

Never say never. AI-based systems making business decisions on their own may not emerge tomorrow or in a couple of decades. It doesn't make sense for businesses to worry about this today. But it will happen, no question. It's a matter of time

Either way, businesses cannot ignore AI's development. Some may decide AI is not right for them, but existing or future competitors will inevitably lay down a challenge with it.

At the heart of our unease about A.I. – not unique to fashion – is a disquiet about the changing power dynamic between human intelligence and the artificial kind. We sense the robots creeping up on us, we imagine them breathing down our necks and we worry about how we will compete. And the more artificial intelligence advances into those areas of our thinking that we experience as creative and emotional, the more spooked we get. Artificial intelligence already guides your car the fastest route home; it probably won't be long until that mapping app communicates with your home hub to put the kettle, music and lights on for your arrival, just like your partner or flat-mate might do. That is intelligence, but it will feel a lot like affection, which we think of as a human-to-human interaction. In the same way, algorithms that know your spending power and established habits already manipulate what you will see if you search online for, say, white trainers. But if one day soon you get dressed in the morning and your phone beeps to tell you that your look is lame, what will that feel like? Cyberbullying?

4. Terminology

Large-scale machine learning concerns the design of learning algorithms, as well as scaling existing algorithms, to work with extremely large data sets.

Deep learning, a class of learning procedures, has facilitated object recognition in images, video labeling, and activity recognition, and is making significant inroads into other areas of perception, such as audio, speech, and natural language processing.

Reinforcement learning is a framework that shifts the focus of machine learning from pattern recognition to experience-driven sequential decision-making. It promises to carry AI applications forward toward taking actions in the real world. While largely confined to academia over the past several decades, it is now seeing some practical, real-world successes.

Robotics is currently concerned with how to train a robot to interact with the world around it in generalizable and predictable ways, how to facilitate manipulation of objects in interactive environments, and how to interact with people. Advances in robotics will rely on commensurate advances to improve the reliability and generality of computer vision and other forms of machine perception.

Computer vision is currently the most prominent form of machine perception. It has been the sub-area of AI most transformed by the rise of deep learning. For the first time, computers are able to perform some vision tasks better than people. Much current research is focused on automatic image and video captioning.

Natural Language Processing, often coupled with automatic speech recognition, is quickly becoming a commodity for widely spoken languages with large data sets.

Research is now shifting to develop refined and capable systems that are able to interact with people through dialog, not just react to stylized requests. Great strides have also been made in machine translation among different languages, with more real-time person-to-person exchanges on the near horizon.

Collaborative systems research investigates models and algorithms to help develop autonomous systems that can work collaboratively with other systems and with humans.

Crowdsourcing and human computation research investigates methods to augment computer systems by making automated calls to human expertise to solve problems that computers alone cannot solve well.

Algorithmic game theory and computational social choice draw attention to the economic and social computing dimensions of AI, such as how systems can handle potentially misaligned incentives, including self-interested human participants or firms and the automated AI-based agents representing them.

Internet of Things (IoT) research is devoted to the idea that a wide array of devices, including appliances, vehicles, buildings, and cameras, can be interconnected to collect and share their abundant sensory information to use for intelligent purposes.

Neuromorphic computing is a set of technologies that seek to mimic biological neural networks to improve the hardware efficiency and robustness of computing systems, often replacing an older emphasis on separate modules for input/ output, instruction-processing, and memory.

22. *Amazon Intro*

The vision of artificial intelligence replacing human professional judgment has arisen many times in the history of the field, and today in some specialized areas where "expert systems" are used to augment or to replace professional judgment in some areas of engineering and of medicine.

"The rise of powerful AI will be either the best, or the worst thing, ever to happen to humanity. We do not yet know which." – Stephen Hawking

Artificial intelligence in literature and movies

- HAL 9000 in 2001 A Space Odyssey
- A.I.: Artificial Intelligence

Artificial intelligence -- mainly its philosophical implications and its impact on the humanities -- is a major theme in David Lodge's campus novel Thinks ... (2001).
- Mike in The Moon is a Harsh Mistress by Robert A. Heinlein
- Neuromancer
- Various novels by Isaac Asimov
- Ghost in the Shell

- The   Matrix
- The Terminator series
- Upgrade
- Zoe
- Tau
- Avengers: Infinity War
- 2036 Origin Unknown

23. Artificial Intelligence & World's Top Universities

Here in this chapter we are going to understand what is going in the minds of top academicians and future scientists of world's top universities like MIT, Caltech, Carnegie Mellon, Stanford, Harvard, Yale, IITs, Cambridge, etc.

Many consider **MIT** to be the leading science school in the world. The many factors that contribute to its success include its location in the Boston area, which locks it arm-in-arm with elite schools like Harvard, Boston College, Boston University, and Tufts. In addition to its association with this prestigious network, MIT boasts 63 Nobel Prize winners and a $16.4 billion endowment. MIT runs several world-class computer research centers, such as its largest research laboratory, the Artificial Intelligence Laboratory. Numerous advancements have come from this lab, including the first credible chess program and much of the technology that was fundamental to the internet. In addition, MIT serves as a leader in nanotechnologies, information theory, and bioinformatics.

Not surprisingly, MIT's computer science department has produced many famous alumni; these include Colin Angel, who founded the IRobot Corporation and completed considerable work for NASA's Mars mission, and William Reddington Hewlett, who co-founded HP.

Stanford has long been recognized as one of the leading centers of higher learning, having produced 49 Nobel Prize recipients, 27 MacArthur fellows, and 20 National Medal of Science honorees. The school also boasts a massive endowment of $24.8 billion. Its alumni have founded some of the world's most recognizable technology companies, such as Google, Yahoo, Taiwan Semiconductor, and Electronic Arts.

CMU has produced many world-class alumni; these include John Nash, whose life was the basis for the popular movie A Beautiful Mind and Professor Scott Falhman, who created the emoticon.

Though the concept of Artificial intelligence has been existing for quite a while, it is only in the recent years that it has picked up on the technology charts and is trending on every industry possible. Becoming one of the best-loved technologies amongst the ingenious minds across the globe, AI demands a blend of computer science, math, cognitive psychology and engineering.

There is no doubt about the fact that soon the demand for professionals trained in Artificial Intelligence would outrun supply. Though there is some overlap of AI with analytics, a proficient AI professional would have deep knowledge on areas like computer vision, NLP, robotics and machine learning.

The scope of Artificial Intelligence was only being witnessed through fictional movies and comics. In today's time, with skillful experts working on this specific computer science discipline, have managed to build devices that are capable of functioning almost like a human. The functions and capabilities of AI are immeasurable, it is believed by several scientists that the subject is in fact a very crucial part of tomorrow because of its wide range of potentiality. AI machines/devices are designed with an aim to produce a human like figure that is capable of responding and thinking. Studying Masters in Artificial Intelligence might be a right choice for you if this subject fascinates your thinking, you might be a great fit to the industry if you can actively participate in improving AI modules by working with large scale organizations.

24. *Artificial Intelligence & Top Global Firms*

Some recent report predicted that global spending on cognitive and Artificial Intelligence systems will reach $77.6B in 2022. In 2018 the market reached $24B in revenue, with the compound annual growth rate (CAGR) for 2017-2022 predicted to reach 37.3%. McKinsey found that 82% of enterprises adopting machine learning and AI have gained a financial return from their investments. For companies across all industries, the median return on investment from cognitive technologies is 17%. Companies competing in the technology, media and entertainment, and telecommunications fields are making the most significant investments and achieving the highest ROI levels. The UK leads all European nations with $7.2B invested in AI and machine learning company acquisitions, private equity investment and mergers from 2008 to 2018.

Apple, Google, Facebook, Amazon, and Microsoft are all working on machine learning and Artificial

Intelligence. Facebook's FAIR (Facebook Artificial Intelligence Research) program engages with academia to assist in solving long term problems in Artificial Intelligence. Facebook is hiring AI experts around the world to assist in their project. Microsoft purchased Maluuba in January 2017, an AI company that uses machine learning for natural language processing. Google Brain is machine learning by trial and error, and Google Translate can translate writings into different languages. AI has beaten the best human competitors in the games Go, Chess, Checkers, Scrabble, Jeopardy! and the poker game No Limit Texas Hold'em.

Companies do not become active and successful at AI through spontaneous combustion. Executives must embrace the decisive role that artificial intelligence and machine learning will play in shaping the next generation of industry leaders and laggards. Managers must recognize that AI's place is not in the future but in the present—and they must act accordingly. In thinking about AI, they must in particular set aside established innovation practices that may well have benefitted them in the past, but which will only hold them back in the future. Future success will require a head-on, fail-fast-and-move-on attitude toward AI projects.

Global top firms like Google, Facebook, Amazon, IBM, Apple, and Microsoft have partnered together to form the Partnership on Artificial Intelligence to Benefit People and Society, referred to as the "Partnership on AI", to ensure ethical, transparent work on AI. AI is being planned to get implemented not just in computers and smart phones, but also in industries such as healthcare, transportation, manufacturing, and robotics. Many futurists believe it is the future of industry.

- Natural Language Processing

- Machine Learning Engineer

- Computer Vision Engineer

- Network Analytics

- Cloud Engineer

- Robotics

Artificial Intelligence jobs are one of most anticipated careers in the world. Top and leading networking firms in the world hire Masters in Artificial Intelligence graduates with promissory packages that are highly impressive. It is an experiential and fascinating field of study approached by individuals with a keen enthusiasm in the field. The world is also excitingly looking forward to AI based devices that are being created and worked on every day under expertise of individuals who have graduated with a degree in AI.

25. Author's Page

Pramod Kumar Singh is an Engineer and MBA from IIT and IIM , numero Uno universities of INDIA. Learning is his passion and he got certified in Contract Law and Finance from Harvard Law School and Wharton School of Management respectively. He comes from a middle class family of Varanasi (Kashi) , a 5000 year old city on the bank of River Ganga. Currently he is based in Mumbai, arguably the most modern city of India. His writings have influence of the blend of ancient Indian culture and most modern tenets of human civilisation.